SAGUARO CACTUS

WEBS OF LIFE

SAGUARO CACTUS

Paul Fleisher

BENCHMARK BOOKS

MARSHALL CAVENDISH
NEW YORK

The author would like to acknowledge Mark Holden of the National Park Service at the Saguaro National Park for his help in researching this book and Paul Sieswerda of the New York Aquarium for his careful reading. The author also thanks his editor, Kate Nunn. And finally, he would like to thank his wife, Debra, for her support in all things, including the work on this book.

Benchmark Books
Marshall Cavendish Corporation
99 White Plains Road
Tarrytown, New York 10591-9001

Text copyright © 1998 by Paul Fleisher
Illustrations copyright © 1998 by Marshall Cavendish Corporation

Illustration by Jean Cassels

Library of Congress Cataloging-in-Publication Data
Fleisher, Paul.
Saguaro cactus / Paul Fleisher.
    p.   cm. -- (Webs of Life)
Includes bibliographical references and index.
Summary: Describes the characteristics and life cycle of the giant saguaro cactus that grows in Arizona's Sonoran Desert.
ISBN 0-7614-0433-3
1.Saguaro—Juvenile literature. 2.Saguaro—Ecology—Sonoran Desert—Juvenile literature. 3. Desert ecology—Sonoran Desert—Juvenile literature. [1. Saguaro. 2. Cactus. 3. Desert ecology. 4. Ecology.] I. Title. II. Series: Fleisher, Paul. Webs of Life.
QK495.C11F58   583'.56—dc21   96-37810   CIP   AC

Photo research by Ellen Barrett Dudley

Cover photo: The Image Bank / Joe Szkodzinski

The photographs in this book are used by permission and through the courtesy of: *T.A. Wiewandt*: 2, 6-7, 8, 9, 10, 12, 13 (top and bottom), 16 (left and right), 17 (left), 18, 26, 28, 32, 35. *The National Audubon Society Collection/Photo Researchers, Inc.*: G.C. Kelly, 11 (left); C.K. Lorenz, 11 (right), 24, 25 (right), 27 (right), 30; Peter B. Kaplan, 14; Tom McHugh, 15, 25 (left); Hiram L. Parent, 17 (right); Van Nostrand, 19; Merlin D. Tuttle, 21; Maslowski, 27 (left); Harold Hoffman, 29 (insert); E.R. Degginger, 29. *DRK Photo*: T.A. Wiewandt, 20; C. Allan Morgan, 22. *Animals Animals*: Leo Keeler, 23 (left); Paul & Shirley Berquist, 23 (right); Raymond A. Mendez, 31 (left); Joe McDonald, 31 (right); Z. Leszczynski, 33. *The Image Bank*: Paul McCormick, 34.

Printed in the United States of America

6 5 4 3 2 1

For Patricia Keeler, illustrator and writing colleague since the beginning.

In southern Arizona, a giant
saguaro (pronounced suh WAR oh)
cactus reaches its arms high above
the Sonoran desert. Look around.
Thousands of tall saguaros are
growing on the lower slopes of
the mountains.

Smaller plants grow in the rocky
soil among the giant cacti. See how
far apart the plants are. In the desert
there's not enough water for plants
to grow close together.

In the winter, the desert usually gets a few inches of gentle rain.

Then in late summer, heavy thunderstorms may sweep across the land. The summer rains cause flash floods. Water roars down the arroyos, creek beds that are dry most of the year.

But for the rest of the year, the Sonoran desert gets no rain at all.

In the spring, if there has been enough rain, the desert plants are bright green. Colorful flowers bloom everywhere.

Small annual plants like grasses, poppies, and daisies sprout from the soil. In just a few weeks, they grow and produce new seeds. Then, as the desert dries out, the annuals die. Animals or the wind scatter the seeds. The seeds wait in the dry soil for the next good rain.

GAMBEL'S QUAIL

ANTELOPE SQUIRREL

Gambel's quail scratch for seeds and small insects among the drying annuals.

The antelope ground squirrel gathers seeds for food. It eats green plants and small insects too.

11

On summer afternoons the temperature in the Sonoran desert can reach 120 degrees Fahrenheit (49° C). The saguaro must survive in this searing heat with very little water.

Plants lose lots of water through their leaves. But cactus plants have no leaves. Most plants use the green chlorophyll in their leaves to make food. The saguaro has chlorophyll in the thick skin

of its stem. The saguaro's waxy skin also keeps it from drying out.

The saguaro cactus gathers rainwater with its wide, shallow roots. They spread out in all directions about as far as the cactus is tall. The roots grow just beneath the surface of the ground. When it rains, the cactus soaks up water and swells to its full size. In dry weather, the cactus slowly shrinks as it uses the water stored in its stem.

DRY SEASON, DEEP PLEATS

Other nearby cactus plants must save water too. The spines of a barrel cactus protect it from being eaten. They also help shade the plant from the hot sun.

The teddy bear cholla (CHOY ah) looks fuzzy and cuddly. But it is covered with needle-sharp spines.

BARREL CACTUS BENEATH
TEDDY BEAR CHOLLA

Pack rats gather pieces of cholla to protect their nests. Pack rats never stop adding to their nests. They also collect twigs, bits of wire and string, and almost anything else they can carry.

PACK RAT

LEAFLESS OCOTILLO

OCOTILLO WITH NEW LEAVES

Leafy desert plants survive in different ways. Some shrubs and trees, like the ocotillo (oh koh TEE oh), drop their leaves when the weather turns dry. The plants look dead. But when the rains come, the ocotillos quickly sprout new leaves.

Palo verde means "green branch." The palo verde tree has chlorophyll in its branches. It can make food without any leaves at all.

PALO VERDE

MESQUITE SEEDPODS

Mesquite and palo verde trees send long taproots into the ground to find water. Many animals rely on the seedpods of these small trees for food.

The creosote bush has an unusual way to get enough water. Its roots make a chemical that keeps other plants away, so the creosote bush doesn't have to share its water.

The giant saguaro cactus begins its life in the shade of a "nurse" tree—usually a mesquite or palo verde. Saguaros grow very slowly. A ten-year-old saguaro may be only six inches tall. It takes many years before the saguaro outgrows its nurse tree.

SAGUARO BENEATH PALO VERDE

The saguaro gradually becomes the biggest plant in the desert. It doesn't grow arms until it is about seventy-five years old. Full-grown saguaros are thirty feet tall or more. They can live for over two hundred years.

A gila (HEE lah) woodpecker pecks out a hole high up in the saguaro. The hole hardens to make a safe nest. The hole doesn't harm the cactus.

GILA WOODPECKER WITH YOUNG

LONG-NOSED BAT

A saguaro cactus doesn't flower and produce seeds until it is about fifty years old. In the spring, white flowers open at the top of the cactus and at the ends of its arms. Each flower stays open for just one night and a day. Bats, insects, and birds visit the flower to drink the nectar. As they drink, the animals get dusted with pollen. Then they carry the pollen to flowers on nearby cacti.

In midsummer, the pollinated flowers ripen into sweet fruit. Animals of the desert depend on the fruit for food. Birds and insects feast on the fruit. Many mammals, including foxes, coyotes, and javelinas (also known as peccaries) eat the fruit that falls to the ground.

People eat the fruit too. The Indians who live in the Sonoran desert make jam and syrup from the sweet, red fruits.

JAVELINAS

DESERT COYOTE

On a hot summer day, we won't see many animals near the saguaro. Most are hidden under rocks, in underground burrows, or in the shade of a plant. This tiny elf owl keeps cool in its nest in the giant saguaro.

ELF OWL IN NEST

POCKET MOUSE

DIAMONDBACK RATTLESNAKE

When the sun goes down, the desert air cools quickly. Animals like this pocket mouse come out to search for food.

Predators hunt mice and other small desert animals at night. The screech owl's large eyes help it see its prey even when there is very little light.

The diamondback rattlesnake also hunts at night. It finds its prey in a special way. It feels the warmth of a nearby animal with a pair of sense organs on its head.

In the spring or fall, when the daytime is cooler, we might see animals searching for food near the great cactus.

Unlike most lizards, the chuckwalla eats only plants. When it is threatened, the chuckwalla hides in a crack in the rocks. It puffs itself up with air so its attacker can't pull it out.

This roadrunner has caught a lizard for its meal. Roadrunners can fly, but they usually run across the desert on their long legs.

CHUCKWALLA

ROADRUNNER WITH LIZARD

Jackrabbits have large ears to help them hear predators like bobcats and coyotes. Their ears also help them keep cool. The blood flowing through their ears is cooled by the desert breeze.

BLACKTAIL JACKRABBIT

MULE DEER

RIGHT: ARIZONA COUGAR
INSET: TURKEY VULTURE

Mule deer browse on the leaves of mesquite and other desert trees.

The mountain lion is the largest predator in the desert. Lions come down from the mountains to hunt deer and other animals.

A vulture circles high overhead. It spreads its wings and soars gracefully on the wind, searching for a dead animal for its next meal.

Let's take a closer look at the desert around the base of the saguaro. It's alive with insects and other small creatures. Butterflies and moths drink from the desert flowers. Ants scurry everywhere gathering food, including bits of saguaro fruit and tiny black saguaro seeds.

Be careful. Scorpions use the sting on their tail to capture prey and to defend themselves. The scorpion's sting can be very dangerous.

SCORPION

BLACK WIDOW

TARANTULA

Spiders hunt, weave webs, or build underground traps to get food. Tarantulas kill insects and other small animals with a bite of their sharp fangs. Female tarantulas can live for up to twenty-five years. Tarantulas are not dangerous to people. Some people even keep them as pets.

31

Are you surprised to see snow in the desert? In the winter, temperatures can drop below freezing. Some animals hibernate, or sleep through the coldest months. This king snake is resting in its hole until the weather warms again.

SONORAN KING SNAKE

Freezing temperatures may kill the giant saguaros. When a dying cactus falls over, insects lay their eggs in the moist flesh. In just a few weeks, the soft parts of the cactus quickly rot away.

In the dry desert air, the long wooden ribs of the giant saguaro last for years. The fallen cactus becomes a shelter for spiders, ants, lizards, and other small animals. And in the shade of a nearby nurse bush, a young cactus is beginning to grow. The seedling is only a few inches tall now, but someday it may be a giant of the desert too.

ANIMAL ORCHESTRA

A Counting Concerto in 10 Parts

Scott Gustafson's
Animal Orchestra

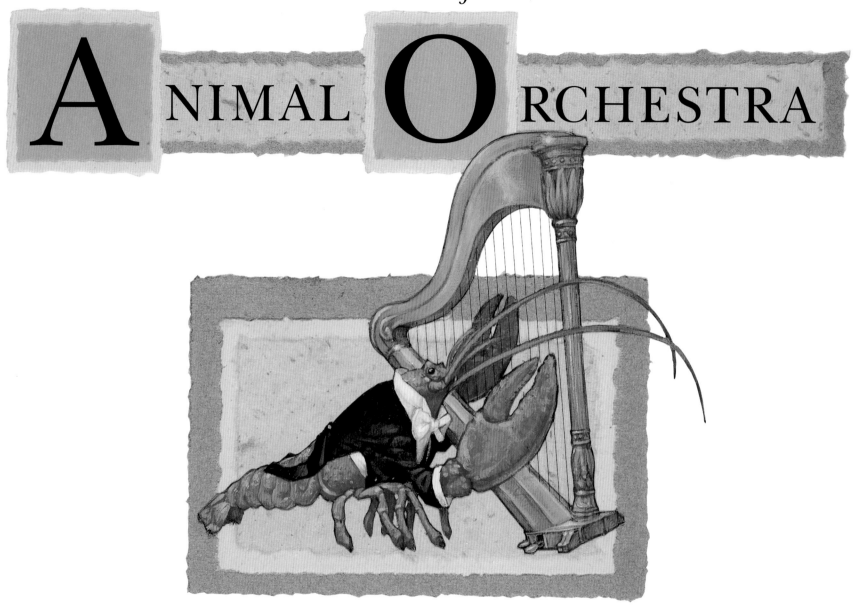

A COUNTING BOOK

THE GREENWICH WORKSHOP PRESS

Shelton, Connecticut

A publication of The Greenwich Workshop Press

•

Copyright © 1995 The Greenwich Workshop, Inc.
Text copyright © 1988 Scott Gustafson
Illustrations copyright © 1988 Scott Gustafson
All rights reserved
Published by The Greenwich Workshop, Inc.
One Greenwich Place, Shelton, Connecticut 06484
Distributed by Artisan, a division of Workman Publishing
708 Broadway, New York, NY 10003-9555

•

•

Library of Congress Cataloging-in-Publication Data
Gustafson, Scott.   (Animal orchestra)
Scott Gustafson's animal orchestra : a counting book. p. cm.
Summary: Depicts the members of an animal orchestra,
from one toucan conductor to ten bestial flautists.
1. Orchestra—Fiction. 2. Animals—Fiction. 3. Counting.
I. Title. II. Title: Animal orchestra.
PZ7.G982127Sc 1995
[E]—dc20 95-22667 CIP AC
ISBN: 0-86713-030-X

•

Manufactured in China
First printing September 1995
10 9 8 7 6 5 4 3

THE GREENWICH WORKSHOP PRESS

ANIMAL ORCHESTRA

To make an Animal Orchestra,
you begin with...

1

Conductor

then add...

2

Double Basses

3
Drums

4

Violins

5
Saxophones

6 French Horns

Trombones

7

8
Clarinets

9
Trumpets

10

Flutes

...Together they all equal

1 Animal Orchestra!

A NOTE FROM THE CONDUCTOR

The following noteworthy musicians number among the finest…
I count on them for every performance!

—Maestro Toucan

DOUBLE BASSES

Ms. Ostrich
Mr. Elephant

DRUMS

Mr. Turtle
Mr. Beaver
Ms. Curlew

VIOLINS

Mr. Rabbit
Mr. Beetle
Ms. Meadowlark
Mr. Squirrel

SAXOPHONES

Mr. Great Blue Heron
Ms. Luna Moth
Ms. Monarch Butterfly
Ms. Spring Azure Butterfly
Mr. California
Dogface Butterfly

FRENCH HORNS

Madam Koala
Master Koala
Madam Kangaroo
Master Kangaroo
Madam Opossum
Master Opossum

TROMBONES

Mr. Moose
Mr. Frog
Mr. Chipmunk
Mr. Mole
Mr. Black-Footed Ferret
Ms. Vole
Mr. Salamander

CLARINETS

Mr. Gibbon
Mr. Hanuman Langur
Mr. Chimpanzee
Mr. Squirrel Monkey
Mr. Gorilla
Mr. Red Spider Monkey
Mr. Maned Marmoset
Mr. Mustached Guenon

TRUMPETS

Mr. Iguana
Mr. Raccoon
Mr. Macaw
Mr. Hedgehog
Mr. Lion
Mr. Groundhog
Mr. Coatimundi
Mr. Otter
Mr. Swan

FLUTES

Mr. Cheetah
Mr. Baboon
Mr. Aardwolf
Mr. Potto
Mr. Aardvark
Mr. Impala
Ms. Zebra
Mr. Hippopotamus
Mr. Cape Buffalo

and
Mr. Skunk